Withdrawn

Fossil Hunters at Work

by Ruth Owen

Consultant:
Dougal Dixon, Paleontologist
Member of the Society of Vertebrate Paleontology
United Kingdom

New York, New York

Credits

Cover, © Zack Frank/Shutterstock and © Kim Steele/Getty Images; 2–3, © Puwadol Jaturawutthichai/Shutterstock; 4, © Michel Gunther/Superstock; 5T, © Photo courtesy of Burke Museum/Specimen held in trust for Bureau of Land Management; 5B, © Photo courtesy of Burke Museum/Specimen held in trust for Bureau of Land Management; 6, © Pascal Goetgheluck/Science Photo Library; 7T, © Puwadol Jaturawutthichai/Shutterstock; 7C, © Phil Degginger/ Science Photo Library; 7B, © San Antonio et al/Creative Commons; 8, © magmarcz/Shutterstock; 9, Photo courtesy of Burke Museum/Specimen held in trust for Bureau of Land Management; 10L, © Bannafarsai Stock/Shutterstock; 10TR, © Krasowit/Shutterstock; 10BR, © Slavolijub Pantelic/Shutterstock; 11, © Herschel Hoffmeyer/Shutterstock; 12T, © Photo courtesy of Burke Museum/Specimen held in trust for Bureau of Land Management; 12BL, © Stockforlife/ Shutterstock; 12BC, © agoindr/Shutterstock; 12BR, © Seregam/Shutterstock; 13, © Dougal Dixon; 14, © ZUMA Press Inc/ Alamy; 15, © Photo courtesy of Burke Museum/Specimen held in trust for Bureau of Land Management; 16, © Breck P. Kent/Shutterstock; 17T, © Tom Connell; 17B, © Kieran Davis; 18, © Photo by David DeMar, courtesy of Burke Museum/ Specimen held in trust for Bureau of Land Management; 19, © Photo courtesy of Burke Museum/Specimen held in trust for Bureau of Land Management; 20, © Photo courtesy of Burke Museum/Specimen held in trust for Bureau of Land Management; 21, © Photo courtesy of Burke Museum/Specimen held in trust for Bureau of Land Management; 22T, © W. Scott McGill/Shutterstock; 22B, © Busara/Shutterstock; 23T, © SimoneN/Shutterstock; 23C, © James Kuether; 23B, © David Herraez Calzada/Shutterstock.

Publisher: Kenn Goin
Senior Editor: Joyce Tavolacci
Creative Director: Spencer Brinker
Image Researcher: Ruth Owen Books

Library of Congress Cataloging-in-Publication Data

Names: Owen, Ruth, 1967– author.
Title: Fossil hunters at work / by Ruth Owen.
Description: New York, New York : Bearport Publishing Company, Inc., [2019] |
    Series: The dino-sphere | Includes bibliographical
    references and index.
Identifiers: LCCN 2018049814 (print) | LCCN 2018053174 (ebook) | ISBN
    9781642802511 (Ebook) | ISBN 9781642801828 (library)
Subjects: LCSH: Fossils—Juvenile literature. | Animals, Fossil—Juvenile
    literature. | Paleontology—Juvenile literature. | Dinosaurs—Juvenile
    literature.
Classification: LCC QE714.5 (ebook) | LCC QE714.5 .O9425 2019 (print) | DDC
    560—dc23
LC record available at https://lccn.loc.gov/2018049814

For more information, write to Bearport Publishing Company, Inc., 45 West 21st Street, Suite 3B, New York, New York 10010. Printed in the United States of America.

10 9 8 7 6 5 4 3 2 1

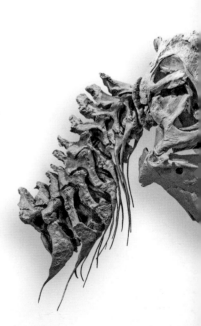

Contents

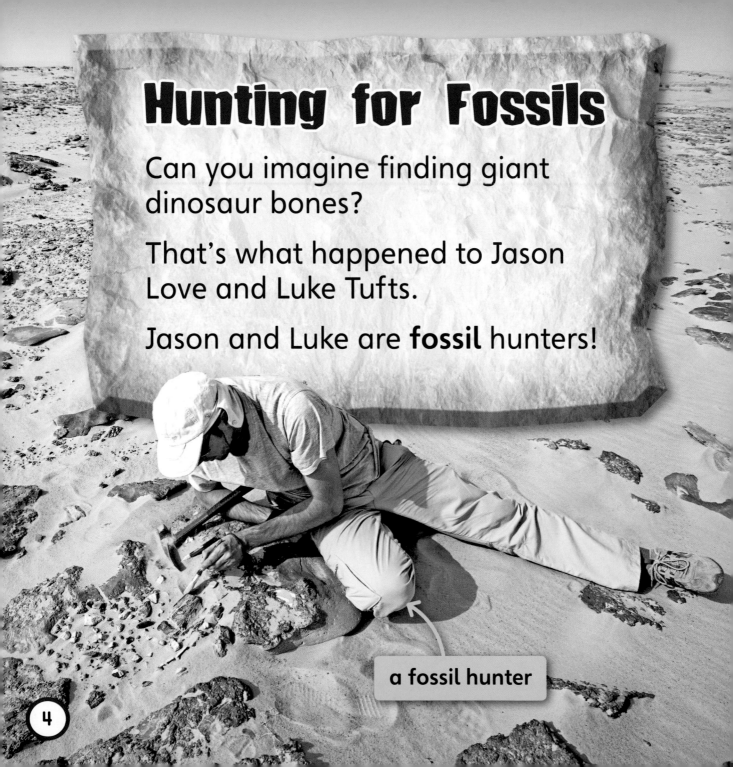

Hunting for Fossils

Can you imagine finding giant dinosaur bones?

That's what happened to Jason Love and Luke Tufts.

Jason and Luke are **fossil** hunters!

a fossil hunter

Fossils are the rocky **remains** of **prehistoric** animals or plants. They are millions of years old.

tooth fossil

bone fossil

What Kind of Dinosaur?

After a fossil is discovered, **scientists** examine it.

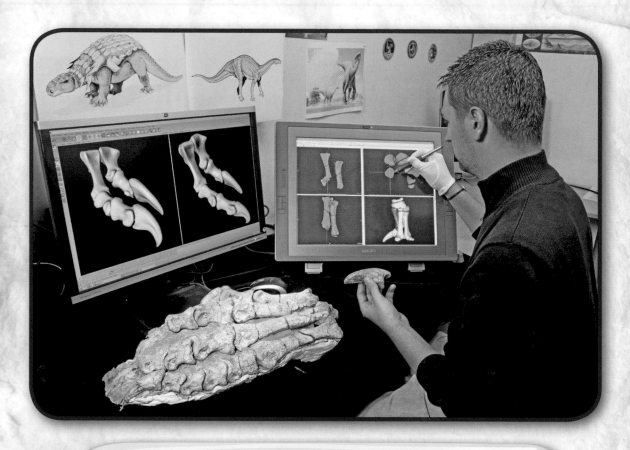

Scientists who study dinosaurs are called paleontologists (pay-lee-uhn-TOL-uh-jists).

They look at a fossil's size and shape and compare it to other bones.

neck bones

jaw bone and teeth

claw

leg bone

The fossil that Jason and Luke found belonged to a big meat-eating dinosaur!

Dinosaur Dig!

The scientists decided to dig up the rest of the dinosaur.

It was located in a rocky area of Montana.

The paleontologists brought tools and other supplies to the area.

They set up tents.

The area where scientists uncover fossils is called the dig site.

tent

dig site

A Big Discovery

First, the scientists removed big chunks of rock from the dig site.

They did this with pickaxes, jackhammers, and shovels.

pickax

excavator

jackhammer

Sometimes, scientists use an excavator to carefully remove rock from a dig site.

Once the scientists started digging, they found more bones and a skull.

They realized the dinosaur was a *Tyrannosaurus rex*!

Tyrannosaurus rex
(ti-ran-uh-SOR-uhss REKS)

Careful Work

Next, the scientists removed the rock close to the fossils.

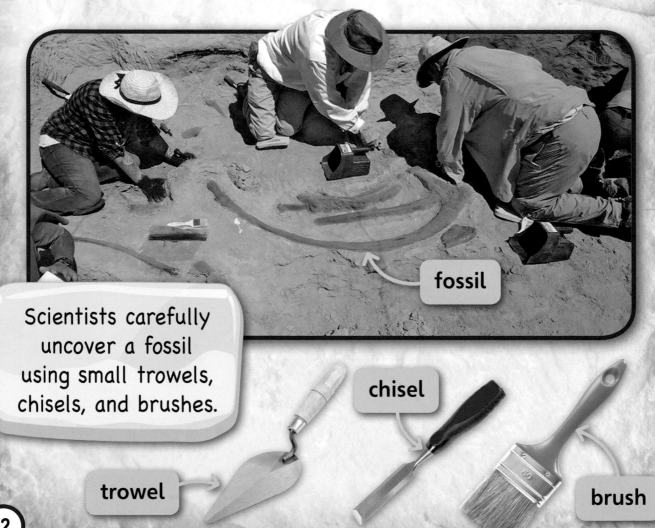

fossil

Scientists carefully uncover a fossil using small trowels, chisels, and brushes.

trowel

chisel

brush

Scientists also drew a map of the dig site.

This helped them remember where each fossil was found.

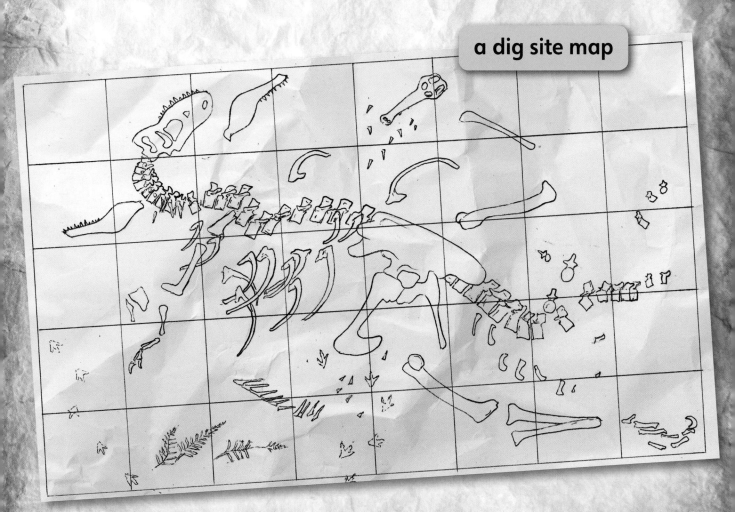

a dig site map

Protecting a Fossil

The *T. rex* skull was dug up inside a lump of rock.

Scientists made a special jacket of wet **plaster** and bandages to protect it.

As the plaster dried, it got hard like a cast!

a scientist covering a fossil with plaster

the skull
inside plaster

Digging up a dinosaur
is hard work. It can be
very tiring and dusty.

Looking for Clues

Scientists carefully checked the rock around the dinosaur.

They looked for other fossils.

Scientists often find plant fossils at a dig site. This helps them learn about prehistoric plants.

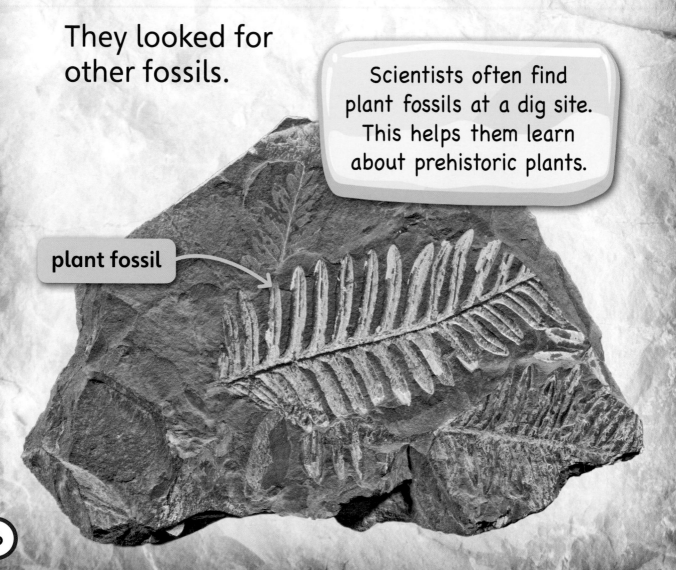

plant fossil

Scientists might find crocodile teeth fossils.

This tells them that crocodiles fed on the dead dinosaur's body!

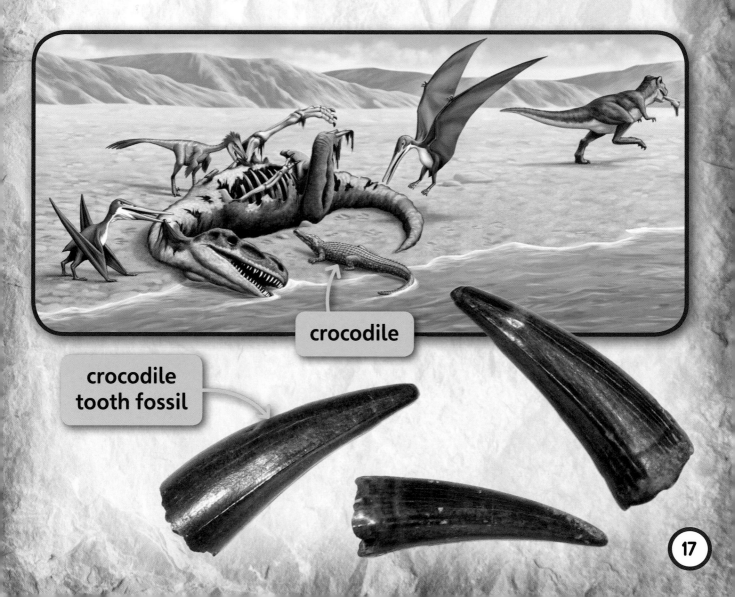

crocodile

crocodile tooth fossil

Off to the Museum!

Next, the scientists used a tractor to lift the *T. rex* skull onto a truck.

Then, it was taken to a **museum** to be studied.

The *T. rex* skull and plaster weighed as much as a rhino!

At the museum, workers carefully cut away the plaster.

plaster

Meet a *T. rex*

Finally, the workers removed all the remaining rock from the skull.

They used small brushes and dental tools.

They also used a tool that blasts sand to chip rock away.

sandblasting tool

fossil

dental tools

Once the fossils were ready, they were put on display for everyone to see!

Glossary

fossil (FOSS-uhl) the rocky remains of an animal or a plant that lived millions of years ago

museum (myoo-ZEE-uhm) a building where interesting objects, such as fossils and art, are studied and displayed

plaster (PLASS-tur) a liquid substance, made of rock, sand, and water, that turns hard when it dries

prehistoric
(pree-hi-STOR-ik)
a time before people
began recording history

remains (ri-MAYNZ)
all or part of a
dead body

scientists (SYE-uhn-tists)
people who study
nature and the world

Index

Read More

Owen, Ruth. *Extreme Dinosaur Hunt (The Dino-sphere)*. New York: Bearport (2019).

Peterson, Judy Monroe. *Fossil Finders: Paleontologists (Extreme Scientists)*. New York: Rosen (2009).

Learn More Online

To learn more about fossil hunters and dinosaurs, visit
www.bearportpublishing.com/dinosphere

About the Author

Ruth Owen has been developing and writing children's books for more than ten years. She first discovered dinosaurs when she was four years old—and loves them as much today as she did then!